INDIE AUTHOR CONFIDENTIAL

SECRETS NO ONE WILL TELL YOU ABOUT BEING A WRITER, VOL 9.

M.L. RONN

Published by Author Level Up LLC.

Version 1.0

Cover Design by Pixelstudio2

Cover Art by jasoshulwathon.

Editing by BZ Hercules.

Time Period Covered in This Book: Q2 2022

Special thank you to the following people on Patreon who supported this book: Zhade Barnet, Stephen Frans, Michael Guishard, Jon Howard, Beth Jackson, Mojo Jojo, Lynda Washington, and Etta Welk.

Some links in this book contain affiliate links. If you purchase books and services through these links, I receive a small commission at no cost to you. You are under no obligation to use these links, but thank you if you do!

For more helpful writing tips and advice, subscribe to the Author Level Up YouTube channel: www.youtube.com/authorlevelup.

CONTENTS

LOOKING FORWARD

ABOUT THIS SERIES

This isn't your typical writing self-help book. This series is a compilation of lessons learned from an indie author trying to walk the path to success. Follow author M.L. Ronn (Michael La Ronn) as he navigates what it means to master the craft of writing, marketing, and running a profitable publishing business. Learn from his successes and failures, and learn about things that most successful authors only talk about behind the scenes.

INTRODUCTION

2022 is shaping up to be a good year for my writing. The second quarter is usually a steadfast quarter—I don't accomplish as much as I do in the first quarter, but the victories are still meaningful. I chalk up the lower productivity to the fact that it's getting nicer outside...and no, I'm not one who spends a lot of time outside. I just produce better when it's cold and depressing.

Spring is always an interesting season because the first half of the quarter is still technically winter; it's cold but slowly getting nicer outside. I lament the change of the season...

Joking aside, I had some personal issues this quarter that slowed me down too—my wife battling long COVID and a family member dealing with cancer. I also dealt with a kidney stone. Yet, somehow, I managed to have a great quarter.

This is the second quarter operating under my streamlined strategic priorities, and I am seeing a big difference. It has helped me to focus more intently on content creation, technology, and data.

My Core Strategic Priorities

As a refresher, my mission is to create content that entertains and/or educates my audience, preferably both, and to remain nimble in an ever-changing industry. I do this by focusing on three strategic priorities:

- Become a world-class content creator
- Become a technology and data-driven writer
- Become the writer of the future (looking forward)

What's in This Volume

In the World-Class Content Creator section, I discuss the value of *The Indie Author Confidential* series, thoughts about the dreaded one-third mark of novels and how to beat it, my experience in rebranding my Good Necromancer and Chicago Rat Shifter series and retiring the M.L. McKnight pen name, and crazy experiments with voice recorder dictation and transcription that exploded my daily word counts and improved my dictation accuracy to around 99 percent.

In the Technology and Data-Driven Writer section, I discuss my first lessons in learning how to design my own book covers, lessons learned in creating large print editions, and my experience with a service that provides helpful market snapshots on the urban fantasy genre. I also discuss issues around pricing books internationally.

In the Looking Forward section, I analyze the 2022 Future Today Institute Trends Report, which outlines major trends that will impact every area of our lives. I also look back at previous volumes of this series to see what was on my mind one and two years ago during this same time. I also discuss a concerning trend with copyright trolls that could impact authors.

Enjoy this volume.

—*M.L. Ronn*
April 15, 2022
Des Moines, Iowa

BECOME A WORLD-CLASS
CONTENT CREATOR

ASSESSING THE VALUE OF THE INDIE AUTHOR CONFIDENTIAL SERIES

Someone recently asked me why I write this series. These books don't necessarily have actionable advice, they're not focused on any single topic, and, to some people, they might be perceived as vain.

I write this series for several reasons.

First, I write it for myself because by doing so, I am more likely to retain the information I learn. If I can articulate concepts simply in 500 to 1,000 words, then I've grasped them.

Next, I wrote this series because of great advice I heard from Gary Vaynerchuk a long time ago. He recommends that influencers and entrepreneurs should "document" their progress and use marketing tools as practitioners of those tools. People will follow you because they're interested in the process and the steps you're taking. That has been insanely true for my writing business.

This series will continue to build in value with every volume I create. Every four volumes (which represents a year, except for the first year), the series quadruples in value. I keep reminding myself of just how powerful a series like this can be ten years from now, or when my career really takes off.

I don't know of a single mega-bestselling author who documents their day-to-day experience like I am doing. For example, I believe it would be immensely valuable to know what Dean Koontz was learning early in his career, especially events that shaped his writing. People would pay a lot of money for that.

Therefore, if I start documenting my progress now while I'm a relative nobody, and I keep it up even when it's not financially lucrative to do so, and if I write honestly, thoughtfully, and intentionally, there's no telling what could happen with this series.

At the time of this writing, each volume of the series is worth $4.99. Every year, I add approximately $10 in value to the series. I do have an anthology collection that pulls all the quarterly volumes together, so I would expect a reader to buy that over the individual volumes.

With the current number of volumes I have published, if a reader bought the entire series, that would gross around $20 if they bought the anthologies (which would net me $14), and $40 if they bought the individual volumes (which would net me $28). That's *per person*, for just the early volumes in this series.

If 1,000 people bought this series in its entirety, that would make me between $20,000 and $40,000.

Traditional publishers would laugh you out of the room if you told them you were only going to sell 1,000 copies of a series. Successful indie authors would laugh you out of the room if you told them you were only going to sell 1,000 copies too.

But here's where they completely miss the point: this is just one series. And sales of this series could help to improve sales of my other titles too.

If I become a bestselling author with a lucrative career, I'll be making way more than $20,000 or $40,000, so this series just adds to my profit. Hell, that money is the equivalent of many people's salaries. Ten years from now, I'll have way more books in this series, and the average value per reader will be over $200.

If I do the same math but ten years from now, if I sell just 1,000 copies of this series, that will between $200,000 and $400,000.

Again, for just one series. For just 1,000 people. I'm assuming that this series will not be a bestseller. If it becomes one, the math changes.

Funny how the numbers add up like that.

Are these numbers delusional? No. Ambitious? Yes. But if I've learned anything over the last decade, it's always to bet on yourself and that success happens in ways that you least expect.

THE PROBLEMATIC ONE-THIRD
MARK OF NOVELS

I wrote a blog post this quarter that resonated with my audience. It had to do with the one-third mark of novels, which is often a graveyard for writers. Here's what I wrote, lightly edited for your pleasure.

———

I wrote 2,000 words today. I'm approximately at the one-third mark of this novel, which is around 16,000 words.

Oh, the one-third mark...it's a serial killer. So many novels die during this patch somewhere between the 25 and 33 percent mark.

I write about the one-third mark in my book *The Pocket Guide to Pantsing*. It's a strange phenomenon that I can't explain other than to say it exists and it rears its ugly head in almost every novel I write. I'm not the only one who experiences it.

The one-third mark is the first point in the novel where you have literally no idea what is going to happen next. You've been on a sugar rush from the time you started the book, and now your sugar levels have crashed. You lose momentum and every word feels like a struggle.

I have a theory for why this happens.

First, many writers would agree that you want to introduce all the key players and stakes within the first 25 percent of the book. All heroes, supporting characters, and villains (to an extent) should at least be introduced so the reader is aware of them. The first quarter of the book, in a way, is about setting up all of this so you can develop the story and characters.

Once you've set the table, so to speak, now all your character and plot lines are converging—hero, supporting heroes, villains, settings, A plots, B plots, and so on. It's like a giant traffic jam and you have to figure out how to unclog the road so that everyone has their lane. Again, for most novels, this hits right around the 25 to 35 percent mark, sometimes sooner. It hits with varying degrees too—some novels (like the one I'm writing) only have small traffic jams. Others have massive ones.

While your subconscious is figuring all this out, it pumps the brakes and your writing output slows down somewhat. Not completely, but enough to where you notice that you can't "see" what happens next as easily. You may have zero idea what to write next and lose confidence in yourself and/or the story.

The novel I am working on now my 37th novel, so fortunately, I've developed some tools to deal with this.

Tool #1 is to write the next sentence, even if you don't know what it is. Follow your fingers. Easier said than done, but it works.

Tool #2 is to take frequent inspiration breaks, such as walking your dog, taking naps, getting away from the writing keyboard and exposing yourself to new people and situations, watching movies and television, and so on. The trick is to look for a "spark," that one thing that your subconscious needs to smooth out the traffic jam and get going again. Find the spark, and the novel will ignite.

Tool #3 is to remember some basic tenets of writing;

1. When the going gets rough, throw a man with a gun in the scene. It works like magic.
2. If the words aren't coming well, write quickly through the current scenes. Not sloppy, but quickly. Don't overthink them—it's very easy to fall into the trap of overthinking. The secret is, when you return in editing (or looping), most of the time, the scene will read better than you felt it did when you were writing it. Always assume your mind is playing tricks on you. When you think something's good, it may not be. When you think something is bad, it also may not be. The best thing you can do is get to the finish line, hire editors, and let readers decide. Readers will often surprise you.
3. Keep momentum every day. Even just a few hundred words is okay. The one-third mark only lasts a few thousand words or so.

The experience I dealt with went like this: I knew exactly what was going to happen for the next three to five chapters, but I found myself in an immediate scene where I didn't know what would get the hero to the next scene.

In other words, I knew what would happen in Chapter A, C, and D, but not B. Chapter B was the trouble.

I followed the tips above and I moved past B into C, and all is clear now. The words are coming back in full force.

Again, don't be sloppy. But don't overthink your writing either.

MAKING CHANGES TO CONTENT
WITH SPEED AND EFFICIENCY

I've talked before about the benefits of thinking about your books as a portfolio. I've documented my efforts in managing my book portfolio extensively in this series. In short, I believe it is critical to know what is going on across your portfolio at all times so that you are never caught off-guard. It is important to be able to make changes quickly because speed and efficiency are one of the key advantages that indie authors have over traditional publishers.

I got to test my preparedness and new workflows with the acquisition of Smashwords by Draft2Digital.

At the time of this writing, I distribute my books through both Draft2Digital and Smashwords. Draft2Digital is a top vendor for me; Smashwords is near the bottom, but I do have readers there.

I've had some gripes with Smashwords over the years. Their interface has always been terrible; even recent changes didn't improve it appreciably in my opinion. For the last few years, I wrestled with turning off the platform entirely for my distribution. Almost all of the platforms it distributes to are reachable through other distributors like Draft2Digital. However, the Smashwords marketplace is unique and worth being in.

In the fall of 2021 after some frustration with the user interface, I decided to turn off all distribution channels on Smashwords except for the Smashwords marketplace. Approximately 90 days later, Smashwords was acquired and it was announced that all books there would be integrated into Draft2Digital's platform. I'm glad I did that in retrospect.

Immediately, when I received the email about the acquisition one morning, I asked, "What's my exposure here?"

The biggest exposure was a messy data migration. When retailers merge books, weird things happen. My main goal was to be prepared for this and stay vigilant for these types of problems.

I was able to verify that all my titles were delisted from Smashwords except for the marketplace. This should insulate me from the worst of the data migration issues. I also use the same email address at both platforms, so there should be no trouble linking my accounts when the developers start migrating data.

Because I already delisted my titles, I can hopefully avoid the messy data migration issues that are sure to follow once the platform integration begins. By *only* having Smashwords's marketplace enabled, I should be able to avoid major issues and keep my distribution business as usual.

Here's what I hope will happen: I will wake up one morning, discover that my Smashwords account is no longer active, and that the Smashwords marketplace shows up as a distribution point for all my books in Draft2Digital. Then, when I log into Draft2Digital, I'll receive a pop-up window that asks if I want to enable the Smashwords marketplace for all my titles, or, it will tell me that this has already been enabled. That's what I'm hoping anyway. In reality, it probably won't be that simple.

That was the first exposure, which I hope will be shored up by end of the year.

The second exposure was that some of my writing books mention Smashwords. Any references to it risk becoming obsolete. I reviewed my portfolio to find all instances where I mentioned Smashwords. In about 15 minutes, I identified four books that contained a potentially soon-to-be obsolete reference to Smashwords. Approximately 45 minutes later, I had made all the necessary updates to the titles, logged the changes in my change log for each book, and uploaded new versions to all retailers.

By noon that day, all updates were published, preserving the evergreen status of those books. (No book is one hundred percent evergreen—there will always be chinks in the armor at some point.)

Because of the portfolio management process I describe in my book *Keep Your Books Selling*, I was able to identify this issue and implement these changes before most authors could even figure out what it meant for them.

This was a great trial run. It's just another sign that the investments I've been making are paying off.

It helps to be organized.

THE SECOND BOOK IS ALWAYS EASIER

A few times a year, I receive a desperate email from an aspiring writer who tells me that they don't know if they can continue their novel. They've never been through the process, they're stuck on the emotional rollercoaster, and it all just seems too difficult to manage.

I know that aspiring writers read the *Indie Author Confidential* series, so I'd like to share my thoughts around how I typically answer this type of inquiry.

First, most obviously, there is already a problem if someone is coming to me. I'm just a random guy who lives in Iowa. What do I know about the personal problems you face? Sure, I've come a long way, and sure, I know a few things about fear and writer's block. But I can't solve your problems for you.

Anxiety is driving you to feel this way. You need to figure out where the anxiety is coming from. Something I've learned over the years is that there are two types of people in this situation. The first type is able to navigate this strange landscape, connect with their feelings, and address them properly. While the process of writing still remains a problem for this group, they have the ability to arm themselves with new skills and techniques so that the anxiety no longer has power over them.

The second type are incapable of addressing this anxiety. I don't mean that as an insult. I mean that they are physiologically unable to stop the bad movie that plays in the theater of their mind. These people need medical and/or therapeutic help. Again, I don't say that as an insult. I say it because it's true.

These people start writing and they come to a spot where they don't know what is going to happen next. Then, the fear kicks in. They tell themselves they can't do it, that their work is not good enough, and other unproductive self-talk. For this group, the self-talk might as well be reality. Their frustration and lack of progress leads them to seek help, which is admirable. But the help they need is not any help that I can provide. And no advice I (or anyone else) give them ever seems to work, which is unfortunate. It's not their fault. Success begins for this group when they admit that they need true help. That should never be a stigma. Personally, I think it's one of the most honorable things you can do as a writer.

All of this is a preface to my answer to the statement "I don't think I can finish my first novel. Help!"

Here's the answer: everything gets easier once you finish your first novel. It doesn't matter how you finish it; it doesn't matter what methods you use—all that matters is that you finish it. When you finish, you will gain a tremendous amount of insight into yourself and how you operate. This insight is impossible to glean when you are writing your first book. It is magnified if you have done the self-work necessary to minimize the inner critic.

The example I like to use is a math class in high school. As a student, I hated math. It just wasn't the way that I thought about the world. Every semester, I wondered if my next math class would be the one where I took home a failing grade.

But somehow, I always made it through the coursework. At the end of the semester, I would look back on the curriculum with pride and tell myself, "That wasn't so bad."

The next semester, when I would have to draw upon knowledge of statistics or algebra or trigonometry or something that came before, I would remember what I learned, and that knowledge would serve me well.

Writing a first novel is like taking your very first mathematics class. It's a different way of thinking, one that you don't intrinsically understand. Like math, you don't know anything about character development, plot, pacing, setting, productivity, and virtually everything else other than what you've read or what someone else has told you (and let's face it—not all advice is equal). You think you know how it's going to go, but you have no idea.

(And if you're a math person, then humor me...I'm sure there is some subject that you dreaded in school.)

Just like taking a pop quiz, a midterm exam, or final exam, you too will be tested at several points throughout your first novel.

Pop quiz number one: how do you actually write a novel? What does it look like on the page? Are you writing prose that looks like what you read in books?

Pop quiz number two: how do you start a novel? Not as easy as you think if you've never done it before.

Pop quiz number three: you're humming along in your novel and you reach the one-third mark, which is notorious for sinking many aspiring writers. I can't tell you how many writers I know personally who have serious struggles with this part in the novel, which usually takes place somewhere between the 25 and 33 percent mark. This pop quiz alone could make you fail the course.

Midterm exam: you've reached the middle of the novel.

Welcome to the murky middle! How do you slog through a bog that you've never been through before? What happens if you show up wearing socks and tennis shoes when you need a pair of waders instead?

Pop quiz number four: what happens when you run out of gas? You've come so far, but now you just don't know if you can continue. Frequently, this is where many of the writers who reach out to me are.

Final exam: can you finish strong?

Those are just some of the pop quizzes and exams where you will be tested during your first novel.

But remember the universal truth of becoming a writer: once you finish your first novel, the next novel will become infinitely easier. How you get there is up to you. Every writer has a different working style. I could recommend many different tactics, but you have to find the method that will work best for you. Just understand that the finish line is the same for everyone. It doesn't matter how you finish that first novel. What matters is that you do.

When it's time to write your second novel, you'll be better at it. It won't feel like it, but you'll have internalized the process so that it won't scare you as much anymore. And for many writers, that will make all the difference in the world—if they have the courage to keep writing.

FALLING PREY TO PERFECTIONISM

This is a story about how I need to follow my own advice.

I frequently teach about how to avoid the perils of perfectionism. Perfectionism is no stranger to writers, and it strikes us in so many ways throughout the production of our manuscripts. We believe that our stories have to be perfect; we feel that sometimes there isn't enough editing in the world that could make a story match the vision we have in our heads; we tweak the formatting of our books endlessly in pursuit of perfection, and so on.

What I failed to understand for myself was just how multifaceted perfectionism can be. I forgot that we are just as likely to become victims of perfectionism outside of the manuscript production process.

Over the last year, I took a break from my YouTube channel. I did this mainly because the pandemic made it difficult to concentrate. Despite being home *all day with access to my video equipment and the ability to record any time*, I told myself that it wasn't the right time.

Why wasn't it the right time? I asked myself that question one day, but I couldn't come up with a good answer.

"It was the pandemic," I said. But as I said, I had access to my recording equipment all the time.

"My editor moved on to different projects," I said.

Video editors are easy to find. There's always someone looking for work. That wasn't an excuse either.

"My videos just wouldn't be at the same level that my subscribers would expect," I said.

That was the answer.

I was so focused on what people thought about the videos that I stopped making them, forgetting the reason why people watch my videos in the first place: the advice.

When I started my YouTube channel, my videos were well produced. Sure, people commented on the nice graphics and the good editing, but at the end of the day, they stayed for the advice and my personality. Somehow, I forgot that over the years.

I realized that continuing my YouTube channel was as simple as sitting down in front of my camera, turning the camera on, speaking my mind, and hitting the stop button.

I knew this all along, but somehow my brain didn't register that I knew it.

Heck, I've built an entire podcast by doing just this technique. My podcast "The Writer's Journey" was me sitting down in front of a microphone and sharing what was on my mind for an hour. So I knew this—I had internalized this.

But I hadn't yet learned this lesson in the YouTube area of my life.

The moment I realized my mistake, I corrected it. I sat down in front of my camera, said what was on my mind, and hit the stop button. Then I did it again. And again.

I am now back to making videos on YouTube, and it has been a satisfying experience. I gave up all of the stress associated with production values. I stopped paying attention to YouTube analytics. I just focused on being me.

Was the content perfect? Heavens, no. That's okay. It doesn't have to be.

So concludes the story about how I have to follow my own advice, and how the things we learn and carry with us often have to be relearned, but on a deeper level.

HIRING A BOOK FORMATTER

When I purchased Vellum, I thought I would never need to hire a book formatter again.

I'm a big fan of doing things myself, especially when they're easy and don't require much time.

I never liked the idea of hiring a book formatter. When I first started publishing, formatters often nickeled and dimed you for every change you needed to make to a book after publication. Even just a few typo changes could cost you. (The nickel and diming isn't as bad now—many reputable formatters clearly disclose when they will charge you now.)

And don't even get me started on formatters who are no longer around due to change of mind, health issues, or death. They vanished and the authors' manuscripts vanished with them.

I believe that you should have unfettered access to your manuscript to change it whenever you need to. Changes could include typos, cover changes, or call to action changes—it doesn't matter what it is; if you have to make it, you have to make it, and you shouldn't have to pay to do it.

That said, I do understand why formatters charge for interior updates because this is a nuisance on their time. I just choose not to go that route.

Fast forward to Vellum, and I have been a happy customer ever since...until I formatted book interior for *Indie Author Confidential Vols. 4-7*. For the first time ever, Vellum produced a paperback file that did not pass Amazon's print on-demand standards. I believe this was because the book was very large (over 500 pages), and Vellum had issues generating the PDF.

I tried many different options, but I could not generate a Vellum export that passed Amazon QA.

I had no choice to hire a formatter because I didn't want a "format gap" in my portfolio. For instance, I didn't want readers to notice that the first volume was available in paperback and the second volume was not. That's not a good look for your portfolio. It's also the very definition of leaving money on the table.

So I hired a formatter. A week later, I had a paperback file that passed Amazon's quality test.

Did I want to do this? No. Was it worth it? Yes, but again, I didn't want to have to do this.

By hiring a formatter, I gave up some flexibility. If I ever want to make a change to the book, I have to send that change to the formatter. I will likely have to pay to make updates.

I was willing to pay this price to support my portfolio, but I will test Vellum in the future to see if I can generate an acceptable file. The moment I can, I am firing the formatter.

To balance some of the loss of flexibility, I made *very* sure that the interior was not going to change anytime soon. This is why I always hire copyeditors and proofreaders for my books, and I make sure that the front and back matter is as evergreen as possible. This way, any changes I have to make should hopefully be minor in nature. If I have to pay a small fee to get those changes done, so be it.

It just goes to show you that everything in the writing life is a tool in your toolbox, and you'll never know when you'll need it.

REBRANDING THE GOOD NECROMANCER COVERS

I decided to rebrand my *Good Necromancer* series. I learned that creating a second pen name for my fiction was a losing proposition. I decided to retire my M.L. McKnight pen name and bring its titles under my primary Michael La Ronn pen name.

I hadn't been happy with my covers for the series, so in addition to rebranding the series, I also ordered new book covers.

The entire process was expensive, time-consuming, and painful—but worth it.

First, I don't want to talk badly about my original designer. He did a great job, and I take responsibility for not being clear in what I needed and not having a thorough understanding of the urban fantasy genre. At the end of the day, it boils down to how good the covers are, and the covers that I had commissioned were good, but they did not convert into sales. That was my fault, not the designer's.

There were a few reasons for this. First, the model on the cover. It didn't look at all like what readers imagined my main character would look like in their heads. I blame the lack of good

African-American models on stock photos sites. This is one reason why it is so ungodly difficult to put people of color on book covers. The models are never good enough, and when you do find a good one, that model doesn't have enough poses to sustain a long series.

Second, I really struggled with how to visualize necromancy on the cover. This is not a dark series, but necromancy is usually associated with very dark overtones. The tone of my series is serious but not dark. It has some elements of humor. The original covers did not convey that at all. I knew it at the time, but I didn't know how to overcome it. All I knew is that I did not want skulls, graves, or dark imagery on the cover. Those things can get your book sandbagged by retailers.

This time around, I wanted to get this right. I engaged with a new designer and did not tell them that the series had been published already. I didn't want to ruin their frame of reference. Instead, I started fresh.

I drew on an important lesson I learned with previous covers: often, less is more when you're explaining the concept to the designer. I explained that the series was about a necromancer who uses his powers for good. I told the designer that necromancy is usually associated with evil, but I didn't want the cover to convey that. Instead, I wanted to lead with a character that people would be interested in clicking on to learn more about. I told them that my main character Lester was a middle-aged African-American man, the kind of guy you'd want to have a beer with. I gave a few details about the plot of the series, but not too much.

The results were pretty good.

The designer nailed the first cover. I couldn't have asked for a better design. Instead of visualizing necromancy with skulls and dark imagery, they instead used another form of magic: an occult magic circle. The designer put it around the main character and made it look as if he was exiting the spirit world. It gave the cover a serious occult, but inviting vibe.

That's extraordinarily difficult to do with a topic like necromancy. All you have to do is say the term and many readers are going to check out. But the designer did a good job in reimagining the series. I knew I was onto something when I shared the cover on social media and way more people commented on it than normal. This happened for every cover reveal I did for the series.

I also discovered that the process of rebranding a cover is way more technical than I expected.

I redesigned the covers.

I also rewrote the book descriptions.

I redesigned the interiors of the ebooks and paperbacks.

I also updated my website with new covers and links.

I purchased ISBNs for each title.

I prepared new marketing materials for the series, including but not limited to ad copy, ad keywords, ad campaigns, 3D mock-ups, social media posts, and more.

I wrote an email newsletter sequence announcing the rebrand. I also had a separate list for my M.L. McKnight readers that I had to integrate with my Michael La Ronn readers in a way that was compliant with email laws. I even inserted a new autoresponder that promoted the series. I also updated my lead magnet for my mailing list to include Book 1 of the series.

I unpublished the old versions, waited for them to disappear, and then re-uploaded the books and republished them at all the different retailers that carry my books.

I lost all my reviews for the series, so I had to use a service to help me gather ARC readers. It sucked, but there was no way around it.

And so much more.

This was by far the most expensive project I embarked on in

a long time. I don't recommend it. However, it was a great learning experience because every fiction series must undergo a rebrand at some point. Fortunately, I won't have to worry about migrating any more titles over to a new pen name (hopefully).

How will the rebranded series do? I have no idea. However, I am confident that I did myself a big favor by moving these titles over now instead of waiting longer to do it. I also followed the same process with my *Chicago Rat Shifter* series, but I didn't need to get that one redesigned. I just migrated those titles over to Michael La Ronn.

Here's why this project will set me up for success in the long-term: instead of having various urban fantasy titles spread out over to pen names, they are now focused under one pen name with identical branding.

The titles under the Michael La Ronn urban fantasy banner are:

- *Dream Born* (The Dream Mage Book 1)
- *Nightmare Stalkers* (The Dream Mage Book 2)
- *Evil Waking* (The Dream Mage Book 3)
- *Shadow Deal* (The Good Necromancer Book 1)
- *Reaper's Way* (The Good Necromancer Book 1.5)
- *Blood Magic* (The Good Necromancer Book 2)
- *Spirit Chaser* (The Good Necromancer Book 3)
- *Mortal Terms* The Good Necromancer Book 4)
- *Death Moon* The Good Necromancer Book 5)
- *Dead Rat Walking* (The Chicago Rat Shifter Book 1)
- *Rat City* (The Chicago Rat Shifter Book 2)
- *Brother Sister Demon Rat* (The Chicago Rat Shifter Book 3)
- *Magic Souls* (Standalone Novel)

That's 13 titles under one name, overnight. I have never had that level of synergy in my portfolio before.

Generally, my fiction efforts until 2019 were scattered. I wrote some science fiction, some fantasy, and some titles that fell in between. I never committed to a genre. Now, when readers find one of my urban fantasy titles and like it, they have an entire playground to explore. This is something I wish I would have figured out much earlier in my career, but we all learn our lessons in due time.

Now I can advertise to my urban fantasy portfolio with purpose. I don't have to worry about bifurcating titles across pen names. I didn't realize how much energy and money it cost me to have multiple pen names for fiction until I rebranded. Now, I truly understand the mistake for what it was.

The actions I took in this chapter will set me up for more growth in the future. Ten years from now, I'm going to be very glad that I went through this.

PRODUCING AUDIOBOOKS FOR MY
ESTATE PLANNING BOOKS

Like many authors, it is my dream to have all of my books produced in audiobook format. It is one expensive dream!

That said, I am always open to publishing books in audio where it makes sense and where I am reasonably certain that I will make a return on my investment. The bigger the audiobook, the more expensive it is, and the more books you have to sell to make back your investment.

When I published *The Author Estate Handbook* and *The Author Heir Handbook*, I knew these books would be good candidates for audio because they fill a niche that is underrepresented. Many authors have thought about estate planning and want to do something about it, but don't know where to start. This type of content lends itself well to commutes, chores, and gym time. It's exactly the type of books I would listen to while doing those things.

So, I put my estate books on my short list of candidates for audio whenever I got around to it.

Around this time, I was approached by the team at Findaway Voices, which is one of the leading audiobook distributors in the world (recently acquired by Spotify). They told me they were launching a new marketplace that connects authors and narrators, and asked if I would be interested in trying it out. They offered to help me find the perfect narrator for the project, free of charge. They also asked me to join them on a livestream to talk about the process in front of their audience.

Naturally, I accepted.

A few days later, the team sent me a short list of very good narrators. They were all professional, had amazing accolades, and if I'm honest, each one could have easily voiced the audiobooks for my estate books.

I chose my top two, and to my surprise, the team at Findaway Voices was able to book those narrators to do a live audition for a sample of my books.

Yes, you read that correctly—the narrators read the text live in front of hundreds of people. Mad props to them for doing that.

Both of the narrators did an amazing job. I had a difficult decision, but I chose the person whose voice felt right to me.

I drafted up a quick contract with the narrator, figured out a few logistics with dates and technical aspects, and a few weeks later, he sent me the first audio files for the book.

Suffice to say that the narrator did a great job. I am very happy with the result.

And now, the inevitable question. The team at Findaway Voices asked me, "Michael, you've narrated your own audiobooks. As much as we want to help you, why did you choose to hire a narrator?"

That is a great question! The answer is that recording my own audiobooks was ambitious—perhaps too ambitious for me. My household is crazy; I have a puppy, chickens, turtle, a seven-year-old, and many obligations to take care of during the day. The only time I can record is between 5 AM and 7 AM during warm months. I can't record during the winter months because that would require me to turn off my furnace, and doing that on a cold winter morning just makes my wife angry.

In short, I don't want to wake up at 5 AM every morning to record audiobooks. I would much rather wake up to write novels. It's a trade-off, but one I'm willing to accept until I am able to go full-time and have a quieter house to work in.

In the meantime, I'm excited to add more titles to my audiobook footprint. I am confident that these titles will perform well. I'll be distributing them on a nonexclusive license to as many places as possible, so I get to play in pools other than Audible, which is always a good thing.

I can't wait for the day that my entire catalog will be available in audio.

EXPERIMENTS WITH VOICE RECORDER DICTATION

Regular readers of this series know that I am an evangelist for dictation. I wrote an entire book on my methods of dictation called *How to Dictate a Book*, so I won't rehash any of my techniques here.

However, I have been experimenting with new ways to dictate and transcribe, and I am excited about my new dictation setup. I want to chronicle the steps I took to unlock a 5,000-per-day (or better) word count.

First, I've been a dictation junkie for a long time. I started dictating in 2016 with my *Last Dragon Lord* series. Not only did I dictate that series, I wrote it into the dark (without an outline) too! Today, it is one of my more successful fiction series.

Back then, I used Dragon for Mac. Dragon for Mac was always the inferior version, and when it was active, Mac users definitely had the short end of the stick. Fortunately, Dragon for Mac was discontinued shortly after I purchased it. However, the Mac version taught me a lot about dictating. I didn't realize that it was less accurate than the Windows version, so I trained myself to speak differently so that the application could understand me better. This took me approximately two weeks, but it was worth it because it helped me learn the ins and outs of dictation like a pro. In just two weeks, I was able to turn my dictation brain on and off, similar to how I turn my Spanish brain on and off when I speak Spanish. Once I learned it, I never forgot it.

Anyway, Dragon for Mac was discontinued and I didn't have a way to run Windows on my Mac, so I stopped dictating for a while.

In 2019, I purchased an upgraded Mac that allowed me to run Windows. I installed Dragon Professional Individual for Windows, and I have been dictating happily ever since.

My dictation journey began with on-screen dictation. This is the dictation style where you sit directly in front of your computer and dictate into a high-quality microphone. Dragon takes your text and converts it into speech in near real-time. This is how I imagine most people dictate, and it is very effective. The only downside to it is that you have to be in front of your computer for it to work, and, if you're like me, you will find yourself using your fingers, which defeats the purpose of dictating in the first place. Still, there's nothing wrong with this method. I used it exclusively for several years.

Fast forward to 2021. I began using Dragon's transcription feature. I would record text at my computer using my podcasting microphone or on the voice memo application on my phone, then I would upload the audio to Dragon. The results were meh. It depended on my microphone; if the microphone was close to my mouth, then the transcription was better, but it still required substantial cleanup. Fiction was pretty much a nonstarter because Dragon didn't recognize proper nouns consistently. At first, I didn't like this method.

Then, I found myself thinking about this again. I thought about additional ways to improve my transcription. I had one week where I was doing a lot of dishes, and I thought, "Gosh, it would be nice to dictate while I'm doing these dishes and get good quality for a change."

The thought wouldn't leave me. Eventually, I came up with the solution.

I have never heard anyone talk about the methods I am about to describe. You can't do a Google search and find what I'm about to tell you on a blog somewhere. No YouTuber I know has ever talked about this, and I certainly don't recall any podcast episode in the author space talking about improving dictation in this way. At best, you'll hear an argument for why you should dictate, equipment recommendations, and some other tips that are more technical in nature.

None of that was useful for me, because like I said, I had a pretty good handle on dictation from the beginning.

Back to transcription. Transcription is amazing. It is by far the most powerful writing technique I can think of—if you do it correctly. The key is that you must do it correctly.

Here's how I did it in a nutshell:

- address the technical issues
- address the editing issues

Addressing the Technical Issues

I purchased a voice recorder. My reasoning was that voice recorders are relatively inexpensive, but the microphones in them have been specifically engineered to capture the human voice. People look down on voice recorders now because the microphones in smartphones are pretty serviceable these days, but my theory was that a dedicated device would help me improve the accuracy of my transcriptions.

I purchased a Sony UX 570 recorder for $70 on Amazon. It's a compact, lightweight, and affordable voice recorder that does exactly what you need it to do and exactly what you would expect: capture the human voice as accurately as possible. In my early tests, I found that the Dragon accuracy rate with the voice recorder was approximately 98 to 99 percent. When I held the voice recorder directly in front of my mouth, it couldn't be beaten. It produced transcriptions that were more consistently accurate than what my podcast microphone could do.

That was the first step, but that wasn't far enough. There are people all over the world using voice recorders and very good microphones, but they still have the same problem: they dictate, transcribe, and spend a lot of time editing. You should know enough about me by this point to know that those words are anathema. I believe in dictating and transcribing cleanly.

The next step was to figure out how to improve the accuracy of my recordings. The better quality of the recording, the better Dragon's accuracy, but that's not the whole picture.

After many experiments, I came up with a concept that I call "the dictation triangle." It has three parts:

- distance to microphone
- diction/articulation
- acoustic environment

Distance to the microphone. No matter what microphone you use, it will record your voice better and with more fidelity the closer it is to your mouth. That's true of a cheap drugstore microphone as well as an expensive podcasting microphone.

Therefore, you need a reliable way to ensure that your

microphone is always two inches from your mouth (or closer). If you're someone who relies on dictation while multitasking, this is problematic. In the case of a voice recorder, it makes zero sense to walk around or drive holding a voice recorder. It's not productive nor is it safe. I prefer to have both my hands free so that I can do whatever I need to do.

For instance, one of the most effective ways I dictate is while doing my dishes. I can't hold my voice recorder with wet hands! That would damage the recorder and make it impossible to clean my dishes.

If I'm doing laundry, I can't hold a voice recorder while I'm putting clothes in the washer. I especially can't hold a voice recorder while I am folding clothes.

If I'm driving and dictating, I'm damn sure not going to hold a voice recorder with one hand and drive with the other. That is extremely unsafe.

So, I devised two solutions.

The first solution was to purchase a harmonica neck holder. This goes around your neck, and instead of a harmonica, you place the voice recorder inside the tension bar. There are felt pads to protect the case. You slip the harmonica neck holder around your neck and then angle the voice recorder so that it is approximately two inches from your mouth. Then, you can dictate hands-free. No matter how you move your body or how you move your head, the harmonica neck holder will hold the voice recorder in a fixed position. Sure, you're going to look a little funny, but that's okay. The increased word count is worth it.

(When I figured out this trick, my wife and daughter laughed at me constantly for an entire evening. Now, they just roll their eyes every time I put the harmonica neck holder on.) The neck holder cost me $20.

The second solution was to purchase an inexpensive lavalier microphone. I paid $15 for the cheapest, best-reviewed microphone I could find. I clipped the microphone to my lapel, which allowed me to also dictate hands-free. This also looks a little better in public! (But honestly, I would go out with the harmonica neck holder if my wife would let me. It's a more elegant solution and you don't have to worry about cables.)

The biggest problem with the lavalier microphone is – you guessed it – cables. I hate cables.

I am not a fan of lavalier microphones for this reason. When I first started recording videos for my YouTube channel, I used a lavalier microphone. It caused me nothing but trouble because:

- the sound quality was poor.
- I had to fiddle with wires.
- I had to arrange the wires to keep them out of
  the way.

The results, while decent, aren't nearly as good as the text from the harmonica neck holder. Dragon gave me around an 80 to 85% accuracy rate. I had to do a lot more editing, but I suppose this is a decent trade-off for not looking like a complete weirdo in public.

But seriously, the harmonica neck holder has no rivals. I've tested transcription in many different ways. It is by far the best.

Articulation/diction. This is how clearly you are speaking so that Dragon can understand you. The goal with this side of the triangle is to minimize as many misunderstandings as possible. The fewer times Dragon misunderstands me, the better.

I watched some videos from trained voice actors and singers on articulation and diction. I remembered the legend of the great Greek orator Demosthenes who put pebbles in his mouth to overcome a speech impediment. He went on to become one of the great orators of his day.

I'm not brave enough to swallow rocks, so I substituted those with a cork instead. I put the cork between my teeth and practiced saying difficult tongue twisters. I also watched many YouTube videos from coaches providing advice on how to improve your articulation.

In many ways, you have to relearn how to speak. You have to think about the speed at which you speak, the words that you speak, your pitch, and even the position of your tongue in your mouth. Very difficult to do consciously, but not impossible.

Environment. If you are multitasking, how distracting is the background? What other resources are competing for the microphone's attention?

For example, as I write this very chapter, I am outside walking my dog and speaking into my voice recorder. It is extremely windy. The wind is a factor in my environment that is making it difficult for the microphone to "hear" me, which means that my accuracy could suffer.

The best way to deal with your environment is to avoid bad acoustic environments or compensate for them. For example, talk louder on a windy day and/or put the microphone closer to your mouth. Or, don't record outside if it's too windy. The time you'll spend cleaning up the text won't be worth it.

That's the dictation triangle.

Addressing the Editing

The next problem you have to solve is the editing problem. As I said, I don't like to spend time editing sloppily dictated text. It defeats the purpose.

I came up with an idea one day while doing dishes. My daughter and I had just been watching Pokémon, and I suppose I had Pikachu on the brain. Around this same time, I was also doing some research on audiobook narration, particularly the punch and roll method. The punch and roll method is a narration style that many professional narrators use to save time while recording audiobooks. Whenever they make a mistake in the text, they stop the recording, rewind about five seconds, and then record over the mistake and continue the recording. It's not the easiest method to learn, but when you do, it saves a tremendous amount of time.

I wondered if I could apply that same framework to dictation.

While dictating, I came up with a stop phrase. This phrase was "Pikachu period." This way, in editing, I could easily identify the sentences that needed to be deleted with a simple CTRL+F. The idea worked so well that I called it the Pikachu Method.

The next problem with editing was interruptions. Since I dictate while multitasking and doing things in public, I sometimes have to stop to talk to people, answer my door, tell my dog to stop sniffing or eating something, and so on. Those sorts of things are no good in a transcription.

Again, I had Pokémon on the brain, so I devised another technique. Instead of turning off the voice recorder, which I was normally wont to do, I decided to keep the voice recorder rolling even when I was interrupted. Whenever I got interrupted, I would say the word "Bulbasaur." After that, I would address the interruption, and when I was ready to start dictating again, I would say "Bulbasaur" again. Then, I would dictate like the interruption never happened. This way, in editing, I could also easily identify large sections of the text that needed to be deleted with a CTRL+F. I just had to look for the Bulbasaur.

I called this the Bulbasaur Method.

Next, I hired a developer to create a Microsoft Word macro that does the following:

- look for every instance of the word Pikachu
- delete every sentence containing the phrase Pikachu
- look for the term Bulbasaur
- look for the next instance of the word Bulbasaur
- delete both instances of Bulbasaur and all text between them.

Less than 24 hours later, I had a shiny new Microsoft Word macro that I mapped to a keyboard shortcut (CTRL+D) that accomplished all these steps in seconds as tracked changes in the document. It cleaned up the text instantly.

When you combine all of these factors together, you have a recipe for extremely clean and fast transcription.

It's worth taking a moment to appreciate just how many things have to go right to achieve success with this unique but crazy effective dictation method:

- You must have the fundamentals of dictation down cold.
- You must be able to do dictation speak (I call it Dragonese) and turn it on and off instantly.
- You must be willing to dictate cleanly and commit to recording text correctly the first time.
- You must have the proper equipment.
- You must ensure that the microphone is always two inches or closer to your mouth, no matter what.
- You must learn how to re-speak so that Dragon better understands your articulation and diction.

- You must be aware of your environment at all times and compensate accordingly.
- You must speak in such a way that you can identify sentences with mistakes and interruptions programmatically.

If you follow these steps, you will get results so good that people will think you are cheating.

This isn't easy, though. It requires commitment, dedication, practice, and most of all, hard work.

This method just isn't for some people. There is always going to be a subset of people out there who read everything I just wrote and say, "This is just too much." And that's fine.

But for those who have the ears to hear it, this method is a game-changer.

If you want to improve your word counts, learn dictation. If you want to explode your word counts, master transcription.

That's why voice recorders are the superior way to dictate. Authors like Kevin J. Anderson have clearly figured this out—I'm just late to the party. You can't beat the microphone quality of voice recorders, and if you let the dictation triangle guide you, you'll have unparalleled accuracy. Best of all, you can write anywhere, anytime, while doing anything.

I have a feeling this method is going to explode my word counts.

I read *The Magic Bakery* by Dean Wesley Smith. I highly recommend that you read the book, but the premise is that you should think of your writing business as a bakery.

A bakery has products: many types of bread, cupcakes, coffee, and more. If you created a bakery that only sold one type of bread, no one would visit. Think about any bakery you've been to; there is a diversity of products. However, it takes time to build a product inventory.

Dean said that, ideally, you want to have around 20 different products before you can expect your bakery to start earning money. That was impactful for me. As someone with over 80 books, I have a hell of a bakery. Or do I?

I inventoried my work to figure out how far along my own bakery is. It turns out I'm not as far along as I'd like to be.

Essentially, I have two bakeries: one for my fiction and one for my nonfiction. You could also argue that I have a third bakery for my poetry, but I'm excluding that for the purposes of this explanation.

My fiction bakery has nearly 40 books. You'd think that it would take off, right? Not quite. I have been a serial genre hopper; I have written science fiction, fantasy, and other genres in between. My fiction bakery is in fact very diverse, but diluted. When I committed to urban fantasy in 2018, that was a step in the right direction, but I don't have enough products in my urban fantasy portion of my bakery. At the time of this writing, I only have 13 titles. I need seven more before I can reasonably expect to see results from my advertising and large portfolio.

My nonfiction bakery is doing quite well. I have over 30 books, YouTube channel with over 300+ videos, two podcast archives, and so much more. But my fiction bakery needs some work.

That's why I am committing to urban fantasy. Moving forward, I am doing my very best to create as many products in this genre as I can. In a few years, I hope my fiction bakery will be thriving. There will be a large concentration of over 20 urban fantasy titles that will bring people in the door. Some of those people will also see my other genres and buy those books as well. There will be an archway in the bakery that opens into my nonfiction wing for those that are interested. Behind the cash register, a television will be playing my YouTube videos and interviews. Okay, I'm taking this analogy way too far, but you get the picture.

Dean discussed much more in the book, like why it is called *The Magic Bakery* and how to think about copyright. Those concepts were helpful too, but the idea of visualizing my work as a bakery was the most impactful for me.

BECOME A TECHNOLOGY
AND DATA-DRIVEN WRITER

MY FIRST STEPS IN LEARNING
COVER DESIGN

It's not a proper volume of the *Indie Author Confidential* series without me bitching about cover design.

This quarter, I put my money where my mouth is and I started learning the basics of cover design. This chapter will summarize my lessons learned.

First, I took a Photoshop essentials course on LinkedIn Learning. I focused on the basics of Photoshop and learning the ins and outs of every tool. Most important to me was determining when each tool was needed. The course offered an ample number of exercise files that played around with.

I have more confidence every time I open up Photoshop now. That's a good thing in and of itself.

I can't say that I am a master at Photoshop, but if I had to grade myself before I started this course, I would've graded myself at an F in proficiency. If I had to grade myself now, I'd give myself a F+. Still failing—but better. I have a long way to go.

The start of the Russia-Ukraine War also reminded me that I really need to get moving on this. My cover designers are Ukrainian. Fortunately, my designers appear to be okay, but there was a period of two weeks where I had no idea if they would deliver the covers that I ordered. I continue to pray for them and their families because I can't imagine what they are going through. I have no idea how they are able to keep designing covers right now—it's pretty remarkable and admirable.

I had to start thinking about what I would do in the unlikely event I needed to switch cover designers. Could I do some of the work myself? One of the files they sent me needed to be corrected.

Also around this time, I started publishing books on Ingram-Spark. I quickly discovered, as many authors who publish their books on both Ingram and Amazon do, that you have to have two paperback cover PDFs to publish on both platforms: one for KDP and one for Ingram. This requires you to pay your designer for two print on-demand files.

I'm always happy to pay my designers for services I need, but this type of inefficiency is against my religion. I thought, "There has to be a way to convert a KDP file to meet Ingram's standards without paying a designer."

I made a job post on Upwork asking for a designer to sit down with me and help me figure out how to streamline this workflow so that I could take the KDP paperback PSD my designer provides and convert it into an IngramSpark file.

Fortunately, this was easier than I thought. The designer and I jumped on a quick call. She showed me how to use the KDP PSD and adapt it to meet IngramSpark specifications every time. I couldn't believe how easy it was.

Let me show you why this was important. If I did the math on all my 80 books to get them into IngramSpark, and each IngramSpark file cost $30 for my designer to create, I just saved myself $2400. That's math you can believe in!

Seriously though, I couldn't believe how easy it was. There

are no YouTube videos, no blog posts, and no resources from anybody that I could find that cover this topic. Learning this saved me a ton of money and served as a good basic education on how to navigate Photoshop as it pertains to print on-demand files.

The designer also showed me how to resize paperback cover files, which is also not that hard. In short, it is easy to increase a paperback size; decreasing it will still require me to hire someone. That is good to know because it means that I should keep my books as compact as possible—it's easier to put stuff in than take it out. That's useful.

That's the extent of my learning this quarter, but every journey begins with baby steps.

SECRETS OF THE DATA MASTERS

I attended a panel from a reputable consultant firm who studied insurance companies and their mastery of data and analytics. It spotlighted the behaviors of a handful of insurers it dubbed "data masters." In short, insurers who embraced data made higher profits and more breakthroughs in innovation.

According to this study, "data masters" use the following external sources to enhance insights:

- publicly available competitor data
- open data
- proprietary datasets from data aggregators
- analyst/industry reports
- data from hyperscalers (like Google, Amazon, Facebook, etc.)
- data from distributors/partners
- social media data
- data from blogs/product reviews
- supplier data
- consumer usage data
- data from platform providers

- anonymous consumer data

"Data masters" synthesize all of these data sources into valuable insights they can use to make informed business decisions.

"Data masters" control large "data estates." A data estate is all of the data a business owns. That's a fascinating concept.

The analysis got me thinking about the same topic for writers.

I believe that data literacy and the ability to use data to develop insights are key skills that writers of the future will need.

If we applied the lens of data mastery to writing, what would it look like?

Publicly available competitor data. Tools like Publisher Rocket allow you to see how other authors are performing with keywords and sales. K-Lytics and Kindle-Trends provide genre snapshots and data about how top titles are performing.

Open data. If you understand APIs, you have access to mountains of data from services like Google Books, Library-Thing, and Goodreads. My Urban Fantasy Database is also another example. You can use this data to mine insights for your genre.

Proprietary datasets from industry aggregators. We don't have too many of these right now. A notable exception was the Author Earnings Reports, but those have been discontinued.

Analyst/Industry reports. I did a quick web search for "publishing industry data." Most of it was behind a paywall, and it wasn't cheap. The cost of the reports ranged from $468 to almost $5,000, which, in my opinion, is outrageous. I got the sense that most of the reports were high-level industry reports that didn't give you detailed datasets, at least none that would give you deeper insights than you could reasonably guess yourself.

I've always struggled with what to do with publishing industry data reports. Personally, I don't think there is much valuable in statements like:

- the audiobook industry is growing by X percent year over year
- traditional publishers reported X million in profit last quarter
- science fiction is seeing growth after a popular series release on Netflix

The data is too high-level to do anything with.

Data from distributors/partners/platform providers. The best example is monthly sales reports.

Social media data. Objectively, you can build a treasure trove of data about readers through effective pay-per-click social media advertising like Facebook Ads. Subjectively, you can browse social media forums and author groups to get a sense of what techniques are working for authors in a certain genre. You can also do the same with readers to determine their tastes. You can weave all of these sources together into a narrative.

Data from blogs and product reviews. This data is readily available.

Despite seeming the opposite, we have a staggering amount of data at our fingertips. It may not all be useful, but it's a start.

That's why I find myself coming back to the same statement: if you want data, you have to create it yourself. As a small author or publisher, you just won't have access to some of the insights that traditional publishers have. The ironic part is that traditional publishers are sitting on mountains and mountains of data, but I don't think they truly understand it. Worse, I don't believe they have the leadership or internal resources to leverage it. Trust me, I know corporate America. Publishers are no different than other industries.

Are YOU a data master? I believe it's something we should all strive for.

KINDLE TRENDS

I signed up for KindleTrends, which is a data service that provides data on the top Amazon titles per genre and how they are performing. It's a useful service because it aggregates publicly available data and saves you time and effort.

Every week, I receive an email with data and analytics about urban fantasy. The report is structured as follows:

- how many new books are in the Top 100
- a breakdown of how many titles are standalone vs. series, Kindle Unlimited vs. wide, traditionally-published vs. self-published, and how many new titles overall were published in the genre
- a breakdown of authors in the Top 100
- trending topics in the genre
- bestseller rankings
- a cover montage and palette of the Top 100
- word cloud with trending most popular words in the Top 100 book descriptions
- breakdown of how many book descriptions are

written in the first- or third- person and how many
focus on setting or character
- links to datasets you can download

It's a phenomenal service that gives me far more insights into the genre than I could glean myself. It also includes an interactive dashboard that lets you filter and sort the Top 100 and 300 titles.

One tip that worked well for me was to scan the book descriptions. I can export all the book descriptions into a single Word document. I scan through those documents and look for any descriptions that catch my eye. It's a good way to study copywriting for fiction.

The only problem with KindleTrends is that it's hard to get a sense of how true urban fantasy titles are performing because many of the Top 100 are paranormal romance titles. In fact, I would argue that the urban fantasy and paranormal romance lists are really just two paranormal romance lists. That's not KindleTrends's fault.

That's why I believe the real action in urban fantasy is happening further down the tail where paranormal romance is less prevalent. If you filter the Top 100 to just urban fantasy titles, they are a minority, and they tend to be closer to the bottom of the list.

If someone did a deep dive at the top 1000 titles in urban fantasy, it would give a much more balanced look at the genre. Paranormal romance would still be overrepresented, but you would see what more urban fantasy authors are doing, and you could determine possible trends based on that. But alas, that is not possible at the moment without significant data work. And it would only be a snapshot in time.

That said, we just have to settle for the tools we have, and KindleTrends is a great one.

PROBLEMS WITH CREATING LARGE PRINT EDITIONS

In previous volumes of this series, I discussed my interest in expanding my portfolio to include large print editions. I recently published large print editions of *The Author Estate Handbook* and *The Author Heir Handbook*. Within the first month alone, I started to see sales for these editions. Nothing major, but noticeable.

I am trying to figure out how to operationalize large print editions so that I can create them with minimal effort as part of my existing workflow. However, I ran into some problems that I don't necessarily know the solutions for yet.

First, Vellum allows you to create large print editions (though flawed), but you have to create a separate Vellum file in order to format it properly. You can't click a box and generate a large print edition in addition to your regular paperback. I don't like that.

The point of a program like Vellum is that you should be able to generate as many formats as you need with the click of a button. This is a serious flaw in their program, and I hope they rectify it soon.

Second, there are common conventions that authors use that

are big no-no's with large print editions. For example, large print readers don't like and/or can't read italicized words and phrases, ragged right justification, and sentences or phrases in all capital letters. Therefore, you must change these formatting elements to comply with best practices.

Both Vellum and Atticus provide tools to help you create large print editions, but neither offers a tool to help you *prepare your text formatting* for large print editions easily (and even then, there are issues). The only solution is to maintain two separate versions of your manuscript, and like I said, I can't stand that.

The best solution I have found for the formatting problem is Microsoft Word macros. For example, I created a macro that changes italicized text to bold. It also flags sentences and phrases that are in all capital letters. However, Microsoft Word macros are not perfect at this, and I have not been able to develop a macro that completely changes all bold text, for example. The macros only get me about 75 percent of the way there.

Third, the paperback trim size. Large print editions generally are printed with 6.14 x 9.21 trim sizes. This means that you have to create a separate PSD file and template for your large print edition. Most designers charge a small fee for this. Keep in mind that you will need to create two PSDs: one for KDP Print and a second for IngramSpark.

Fourth, there's the problem of distribution. If you want to do large print editions correctly, you need to have a large print edition on KDP and one on IngramSpark.

KDP only allows you to link one version of your paperback and hardcover to your ebook edition. This means that 1) your large print edition will be out there "floating" on your dashboard, 2) you will have two separate versions of the book, and 3) whichever format you don't link will be difficult for readers to find.

At the time of this writing, Amazon doesn't like large print editions. If a book has an ebook, trade paperback, hardcover, or audiobook edition, you will see them prominently above-the-fold on the sales page. If that same book has a large print edition, you have to click on a button that reveals additional formats. And even then, the large print edition shows up as "paperback." The only way a reader will know if a book is large print is if the author puts the words "large print" in the title, book description, copyright page, and the book cover. Otherwise, they might not notice.

Amazon also doesn't like IngramSpark. If you distribute to Amazon from IngramSpark, it's not uncommon that your title will show as out of stock, or the shipping will take longer. Instead, they prioritize products carried by their own facilities. This is why you must publish large print editions to both Amazon and IngramSpark.

Add all these factors together and you have many headwinds in creating large print editions right now. That's precisely why I am interested in jumping into the format now. This is what things look like before retailers innovate. I'm willing to bet that, several years from now, it will be much easier to create these editions. I'll benefit from having figured all of this out now.

FIXING A CHAPTER TITLE ISSUE

Earlier this quarter, I discovered an embarrassing quality error. This type of error is precisely why I have instituted quality checks for my books. Sadly, my QA process would have missed this error and I only uncovered it out of sheer luck.

I created my very first large print edition for my book *The Author Estate Handbook*. This also happened to be the first book I ever published through IngramSpark, so I purchased an author copy.

The copy arrived in the mail, and I was satisfied with the quality, book cover, pages, and so on. As far as author copies go, it was a fine specimen.

However, to my surprise, I thumbed to a random page and noticed that something was wrong with the header. The chapter title was truncated. Instead of saying "ABCDEFG," it said "ABCDE..."

Seeing that was a punch to the gut. I stopped everything I was doing and immediately inventoried which of my books have chapter titles in the headers. Fortunately, the only books in my catalogue that have chapters in the title are the *Indie Author Confidential* series.

It turns out that if your chapter title is greater than 35 characters, then Vellum will truncate it. You would think that Vellum would prevent this from happening by warning the user. It does not.

This is a critical quality error, and one that could easily be missed under the right circumstances (like mine). Most authors don't order proofs if they trust their designer and have been doing this for a long time (like me). The only reason I ordered this proof was because it was my first voyage at IngramSpark. If I hadn't done that, I wouldn't have noticed this for a very, very long time.

Of course, I take responsibility. But this would be an easy thing to address programmatically in an app. Just sayin'.

I fixed this problem once and for all. I identified three books in this series that had the truncated header problem. I contracted a developer to write a Microsoft Word macro. This macro identifies chapter headings, counts the number of characters in the chapter title, and inserts a comment with a warning for any chapters that exceed 35 characters. Problem solved. I made the change to all of the books, reuploaded them, and took a big sigh of relief.

If you haven't checked your proofs in a while, maybe you ought to do it more frequently. I have decided to check the proofs for Book 1s in series and every fifth nonfiction book. I still think it is overkill to check proofs for every title (and expensive), but I don't want to be surprised like this again if I can avoid it.

THE MORE THINGS CHANGE, THE MORE THEY STAY THE SAME

The more things change, the more they stay the same. I was talking with an author recently about the progress of technology in the writing world. We were talking about writing on your phone.

This author (who was a few decades older than me) talked about how writing on your phone was actually a thing before it was a thing. She explained that she used to have a PDA and how she could write text on them via an app. She could then upload that text to a computer and convert it to a text file or a Microsoft Word file. This would have been perfect back then because most people who were writing any kind of manuscripts were probably using Microsoft Word or WordPerfect anyway.

I like to think that if I were an author in the 90s or early 2000's, I would have discovered this hack.

But it just goes to show you that the more things change, the more they stay the same. There is always a will and a way for those who want to improve their word counts.

ESSENTIAL COMPUTER SKILLS FOR WRITERS

I read an article about essential computer skills for writers. It said that writers needed to have a professional-looking email address, not share an email with a spouse, and they needed to observe email etiquette. They also needed to learn Microsoft Word.

I agree with those suggestions, but they're woefully inadequate. This was true in 1997.

Today (at the time of this writing) is 2022 and the world has changed.

Here are the skills that writers in today's age need, and it's more than just email skills and Microsoft Word. These skills are not just required; they get you in the door. In other words, you can't expect to have a successful career unless you master them at some level. These skills are merely the cost of competing—we won't go into advanced concepts like pay-per-click advertising or copyright.

Microsoft Excel. You also knew I was going to say this.

Email productivity. Sure, you need to know email basics, but you also need tools to help you destroy your inbox with ruthless efficiency. Email controls our lives whether we admit it or not, and we have to deal with it. If you can't manage your emails swiftly, you'll potentially miss out on opportunities, and you may miss issues that are happening across your portfolio.

Email marketing. Knowing how to build a list, segment that list, write good copy, and create engaging autoresponders will be more important than ever.

Basic data analysis. The future belongs to the writers who will become data masters, but knowing how to analyze things like your sales and market trends are becoming increasingly important. Authors are not generally numbers people, so this will be a disadvantage to many.

Teleconferencing skills. If you can't run or participate in a video call at this point, you're in trouble.

Audio/visual production and editing. Knowing how to edit audio and video is a critical skill in a world that religiously consumes multimedia content like videos and podcasts.

Media interviews. I don't care how much of an introvert you are; knowing how to give a good interview or media appearance is important.

Hiring work. No one can do everything. You will need to hire people to help you with one-off tasks. You would be surprised at how many people struggle with this. The key is to articulate succinctly and efficiently exactly what you need so that you eliminate any back-and-forth. Your goal should be for any freelancer you hire to complete the work on the first try or second try with minimal revisions. This is easier said than done and requires experience.

Book formatting. Even if you use software like Vellum or Atticus, you still need a basic understanding of ebook and print layout.

Cybersecurity. You need to know how to avoid malware,

random attacks, and other acts by bad actors. Otherwise, you could expose your writing business to hackers.

Website creation and maintenance. Most people use WordPress. Whichever content management system you use, you must master it. You must also understand how to navigate the underbelly of website hosting in case you become a victim of an attack.

Are those the only skills writers today need? Heavens no, but it's a good start.

EFFICIENT CAPITAL

What does a more efficient writing business look like? I don't mean writing better or faster. I'm purely talking business here.

Most people would look at the money coming in and going out. Expenses are certainly one way to think about this problem; they have a wonderful way of hiding inefficiencies.

I define efficiency as being able to operate such that you obtain a profit faster than your competitors.

If you review your expenses, the key question you should ask is "how can this expense pay for itself?" To me, that should be the North Star of creating an efficient writing business. Every dollar that comes in should work much less than the average author's.

Let's go through the different categories of expenses and figure out how they could pay for themselves.

Website domain and hosting. These cost an average of $200 per year. Do you sell books directly on your website? If so, that can easily defray some of the hosting costs each year. Direct sales grow over time. What if you also allocated your Amazon Associates commissions and other affiliate link income to your website? What if you could rig it so that your website domain and hosting are technically free each year?

Costs of book production. Until recently, I didn't think there was a way to defray these costs outside of having a Patreon or similar service. However, Kickstarter has changed the math considerably. More and more authors are using Kickstarter to fund their novels. After Brandon Sanderson's amazing success, that number is only going to change. This quarter, I backed a novel by Kevin J. Anderson that earned over $5,000. I've only corresponded with Kevin once or twice, but I can guarandamntee you that it didn't cost him $5,000 to produce the ebook and paperback versions of the novel. I'd be shocked if that cost more than $1,000. The Kickstarter campaign basically allowed Kevin to produce his novel for free, at a profit.

Imagine running a successful Kickstarter campaign a few times per year. It could effectively zero-out your business's expenses, even after taxes...

Advertising. Can you write good ad copy and learn pay-per-click advertising so that your ads generate a profit each month? Could you tweak your ads so that you decrease wasted ad spend as much as possible? That's the pathway to efficiency here.

Annual business costs. Things like PO boxes, Secretary of State filings, and other legal fees can't be defrayed, but if you do them correctly, they don't cost very much anyway. I pay $225 per year for my mailbox, $150 per year for a registered agent service, and $85 every other year for my Secretary of State filing. That's $460 per year just to operate my business. Not bad, especially if I can make almost every other area of my writing business efficient. I can't think of many businesses that can operate for less than $500 a year. That is a blessing for authors that not enough of us appreciate.

Next, some data analysis. If I created a spreadsheet with my expenses in Column A, the amount of money recouped in Column B, and the amount offset in Column C, I'm curious what the total number would be. If I can drive that number down to the lowest possible (without being ridiculous about it), that number is my competitive advantage.

Think about it: Author A spends $10,000 in expenses per year. Author B allocates their expenses to income and spends $10,000 as well, but through allocation, they're *technically* only spending $4500. They have more money in their bank account at the end of the day and can use that to pursue additional advantages, whereas Author A's money will be far more inefficient. And, most importantly, everything Author B earns over $4500 is pure profit, so they arrive at a profit much faster (and more efficiently).

Making your business more efficient is a beautiful thing.

PITFALLS WITH INDIE AUTHOR PRICING

Recently, I was working with a fellow writer on developing a resource that people could use to price their books better in international currencies.

I see this is one of the great problems that we face as writers.

How should you price your book? There are many factors to consider that make this a Rubik's cube of a problem:

- country
- format
- genre
- length
- economic considerations like the cost of printing a paperback or producing an audiobook)
- reputation of the author
- retailer
- venues such as libraries
- how traditional publishers are pricing their books
- and more

My opinion (and I seem to be alone in thinking this) is that authors need to be told what to price their books. They don't want to or have time to weigh all these factors, and they certainly don't want to have to keep all this straight. I've talked to people who believe a book should be priced differently at different retailers; I don't know if that's right or wrong, but most people I know don't have systems in place to track or monitor a strategy like this. It takes a lot of skill and effort.

Again, that's why I think people just want a number. It's not useful or productive to give them a big range. People just want to know what to put in the box.

The best thing someone can do for the community is embark on an intensive research project in at least the major currencies of the world (USD, GBP, EUR in its major variations, CAD, AUD, and a few others). This research would encompass how books are priced, reader habits and considerations, and additional competitive analysis to figure out how traditionally published authors are pricing versus self-published authors. This research should become the basis of a recommendation.

That recommendation should be in the form of a database with one-to-one mappings of currencies. Ideally, an author could go to this database, select their home currency and other attributes such as genre or format, and then get an instant list of recommendations for price points in all major currencies. $4.99 USD would equal £3.99 GBP, €4.99, and so on. The author could save that spreadsheet to their computer to reference when publishing a book. Or, they could use it as a starting point and tweak it from there.

But this would require a lot of work. I almost embarked on this project myself, but I determined that it wasn't worth it right now.

LOOKING FORWARD

ANALYZING THE 2022 FUTURE TODAY INSTITUTE REPORT

The Future Today Institute released its 2022 Trends Report. If you're not familiar with FTI, you should be, as their reports are must-reads. I usually stop what I'm doing to read the reports the moment they come out. This year is 668 pages of future trends that will shape our society. Wow—no mere mortal can read all of this, but I like to scan the digest to see if there are any trends that will potentially impact my writing business.

Here are my takeaways.

Synthetic media will be used to generate popular likenesses to deliver a range of personalized products and services at scale.

Synthetic media is any software that uses AI to generate content. Right now, you see it in apps that generate art based on a description you enter (especially on Twitter with people generating art based on Taylor Swift song lyrics, for example).

The team at OpenAI released a demo of a program called DALL-e, which takes this to the next level.

In DALL-e, you type in a sentence that describes the image you need, like "a chair that looks like an avocado" or a "tiny radish walking a dog." DALL-e then generates a panel of images that are inspired by what you wrote. And wow, the images are surprisingly good. Look it up.

This will be the future of stock images. Imagine browsing Shutterstock and you can't find the image you need. Click a button, tell Shutterstock what you want, and it will generate some options. Click the one you want, pay for a license, and boom. You will literally be the only person in the world to have that image. Why does Shutterstock need content creators, then? (I'm not advocating for this, just making an observation).

More specifically, DALL-e can even generate clothing renders. I saw one example where the user asked for a mannequin wearing a checkered flannel shirt. It generated several options in several poses. I could change the clothes on the mannequin with a click of a button.

The next-next level is being able to generate faces that go on that model, and customizing those faces... and then you'll literally be able to type in a description of your main character, get a character render, and then be able to use that on your cover royalty-free. This will be great for authors like me who struggle to find models of color. I'd be very nervous if I was a vector artist or stock photography model, though.

Face generation technology does exist and it's quite good, but I haven't seen anyone bring the two pieces of tech together yet (synthetic art + synthetic faces, bodies, and poses). When that happens, the game will change.

But more importantly, this will fundamentally change how cover designers work. It will enable them to create better covers that match both theirs and the author's visions. The downside is that the designers who specialize in compositing will find their skillset less in demand as these types of apps proliferate. I'd also be nervous if I was a compositor.

More practically, imagine writing a blog post and needing an image. Open a WordPress plugin, tell it what you need, and boom, you've got a beautiful, high-quality image for your blog that will keep readers engaged.

Companies are looking to upskill their workforce in machine learning and the basics of AI.

If companies are looking to do this, then we should be too. What skills should every author know twenty years from now? Figure that out and start learning today.

A few skills that I think are critical to have at least basic proficiency in would be data literacy (being able to look at data and make accurate decisions based on what the data says), basic programming understanding (Python, Java, and so on), and cybersecurity best practices. Those are a great start.

Some skills that are key right now will remain key in the future: copywriting, storytelling, knowing how to run your finances, and so on.

If you don't upskill, you're going to get left behind.

Until about 2007, the skills an author needed were pretty basic—they needed Microsoft Word proficiency, storytelling prowess, contract negotiation skills, and basic marketing skills. Then, the advent of self-publishing came along and authors had to add Internet savviness, book formatting, cover design, and more to their skillsets. The advent of AI and machine learning becoming mainstream and woven into the fabric of everyday lives will require them to become even more adept.

If you don't like it, be ready to get left behind.

There are plenty of sites that can teach you basic skills quickly. Coursera, LinkedIn Learning, Skillshare, and Udemy are a few. Unlike in the past, the information is out there.

To paraphrase Wayne Gretzky, you just have to figure out where the puck is headed, educate yourself, and then start small. I'm not advocating for people to become programmers or AI scientists—but you do have to understand how to speak the language.

Machine learning is transitioning, as new platforms allow businesses to leverage the power of AI to build applications without the need to know specific code.

As more developers become comfortable with AI, they'll start offering more AI services to the author community. At some point, I expect writing apps to be interlaced with AI capabilities, and that's where folks will have to be careful.

What those services will be, I don't know, but a critical skill in the future will be to understand how your data is going to be used.

If someone wants to scan your manuscript to give you insights, your data will almost certainly be used for other purposes. In an age of AI, you'll have to weigh whether it is worth it and what the benefits potentially are. There will be a lot of small startups and companies trying to offer new technology, but not all of them will succeed. You should be very selective who you give your data to because it's akin to giving them money. I forget who said that giving your data to an AI company is like investing in them, and you get paid with the benefits of the service rather than money. I think that's a wise way to think about new AI tools instead of "Wow, this is free! How cool!"

People will create multiple digital versions of themselves, each tailored for specific purposes. This will lead to fragmentation—and a widening gap between who a person is in the physical world, and who they project in various online platforms.

If you thought reaching readers was hard now...

This will completely disrupt advertising. Instead of advertising to people, you'll be marketing to their avatars, which will make it much harder to determine buying habits and behaviors.

The flip side is that people could create avatars that are easier to market to. I could create an avatar that is all about urban fantasy, for example. Maybe I WANT that avatar to be advertised to with UF books and new authors.

But there will inevitably be people who become harder to reach in a fragmented world. Some of those people are people who we're currently advertising to. Like I said, I think PPC advertising's days are numbered in its current form. I have no idea what will replace it, but if you're one of those authors who derives much of your income from advertising, I'd start diversifying now. Some good ideas: direct sales, Kickstarter, investing in your email list, going wide, getting into audio, etc. There are lots of choices.

. . .

Ransomware will become the new "smash and grab" of cybercrime.

I've been saying this since early 2020, and that was before attacks started spiking. It's a wise idea to educate yourself on cybercrime and how to protect yourself and your business.

China will push for the broader use of its digital currency, the e-CNY, within and outside of the country.

This idea will spread all over the world, with many countries instituting their own digital currencies. Every transaction will be tracked. The ramifications of this are scary: if you think cancel culture is bad now, wait until the government starts monitoring your transactions and blocks you from purchasing certain things from certain people for any reason. Such a scenario will make the current moment of heated cancel culture feel like the good old days.

If you're a writer writing erotica, for example, and a state government doesn't want its citizens to purchase erotica, they could freeze you out. Or, if you're writing work that is political or challenging to the status quo in any way, you could be targeted.

To get around this, I predict that people will use alternative forms of currency like crypto to purchase disfavored items.

Blockchain-based applications are being used to track the origins of content online, and permanently store original assets, improving the ability of consumers and businesses to authenticate infor-

mation. This is a powerful tool for combatting censorship and misinformation.

In the future, no one will know what is real and what is false, and no one will really care as until they need to care. That's scary. There will be no such thing as a shared historical experience. Up until now, everyone grew up consuming the same media and was exposed to the same cultural items. That won't be true of children born from now. Everything is going to be fractured, with individuals and populations having their own fragmented experiences.

From a consumption standpoint, there were so many books I wish I would have known about when I was younger. I would have devoured them. Readers will live in a future where every book recommendation is optimized. Which books get recommended and which ones don't?

Those are a few of the takeaways that I'm watching closely. I look forward to reading next year's report.

LOOKING BACK

This volume represents the first volume where I can look two years into the past. I started the *Indie Author Confidential* series in Q2 2020, so I thought it would be fun to start a new recurring segment that looks at the previous years at the same point in time to see what I was discussing and how it panned out.

What was I discussing this time one year ago? Two years ago? *Five* years ago?

One Year Ago - Q2 2021

Become a World-Class Content Creator

The 5-5-50,000 Challenge. I tried a crazy challenge where I tried to write 5,000 words per day for 10 days to achieve a 50,000-word novel. I failed tremendously. I still think I would fail today if I tried it, though my voice recorder hack would help me get closer to a 5,000-word quota. I'd like to try this sometime in the future, but not any time soon.

Complaining About ISBNs. This time last year, I said I would not buy ISBNs. Funny how things change quickly! To be fair, the only reason I ultimately purchased them was because my accountant told me to make some big purchases by end of year to minimize my tax liability.

Livestreaming Experiments. This time a year ago, I hit my stride with my "Power Hour" livestreams. It started on a whim and I didn't think anyone would be interested. They turned out to be a huge hit, and I've been doing them every month ever since.

The Looming Cover Designer Shortage. For the first time in this series, I predicted the cover impending cover designer shortage. It hasn't happened yet, but as I wrote in later volumes, the prices of cover designers skyrocketed again *after* I wrote about it. We're in for a rude awakening at some point in the very near future.

Become a Technology and Data-Driven Writer

The Importance of Being Nimble. I wrote about slipping in my driveway on a patch of black ice and how that got me thinking about the critical need to learn how to write in alternative methods. For instance, if you break your wrist, you aren't doing any typing for a while. Knowing how to dictate can keep you productive while you're healing. My experiments with dictation, transcription, and writing on my phone continue to help me insulate myself against being unable to write. As of now, I can write anywhere, any time, and in any position. That's one of my strategic advantages.

Deepfakes. The Tom Cruise deep fake came out around this time, and I wrote about how scary it was. There hasn't been much deep fake activity since, at least none that have caught my eye.

Two Years Ago - Q2 2020

Become a World-Class Content Creator

Writing with the Audiobook in Mind. Writing a novel is hard enough; it's easy to forget about tricks that help you write for audio. I was onto something. Earlier this year (2022), I spoke with a company who is developing a tool to help writers with this issue. The software scans a manuscript and alerts authors to potential troublespots for narrators. I really hope the company succeeds. I was definitely ahead of the curve on this one.

Become a Technology and Data-Driven Writer

Ransom Attacks. If you need any proof that I was one of the first people in the indie author community talking about ransom attacks, mark Q2 2020 down and see if anyone said anything about it earlier than that. Here's what I wrote: "Ransom attacks are on the rise. I talk about this exposure at length in my course *Writing in Hard Times*. I believe it is an emerging threat for writers, but I don't talk about it publicly for fear of bad guys hearing it.

"A ransomware attack is when a cybercriminal gets access to your computer and then shuts it down and makes you pay money to get access back.

"Many people think ransomware attacks only happen at large organizations. I've read industry statistics that somewhere around 60-70% of ransomware attacks are actually on small businesses.

"Writers are small businesses. In fact, we're what the industry calls "micro small businesses."

"It's just a matter of time before ransomware creators realize that self-published writers are worthy targets, so start preparing now."

Anyway, now it's 2022 and ransom attacks are still on the rise. Start protecting yourself now because it's going to become a serious problem for authors.

My immediate recommendations:

- Educate yourself on cybersecurity.
- Install antivirus software on your computer.
- Keep your website and any website plugins up-to-date.
- Use a password manager to protect your accounts.
- Use two-factor authentication wherever and whenever possible.
- Back up your work in multiple places so you can recover your backups.
- Use a backup service like Backblaze to create secure, time-stamped backups.
- Use an encryption service like BoxCryptor to protect any files that you store in the cloud.
- Consider cyber liability insurance.

I'm very careful not to share these tips publicly because I don't want to draw too much attention to this issue. If you're reading this, you're lucky because outside of my *Writing in Hard Times* course, I have never shared my recommendations publicly.

Be careful out there!

Become the Writer of the Future/Looking Forward

Four Areas Where AI Can Help Writers. I wrote that there were four areas that authors could benefit greatly from AI:

1. Developmental editing
2. Writing assistance
3. Marketing assistance
4. Writing to market

Have there been any developments? Not quite. There is promise with writing assistance apps—Sudowrite is gaining popularity and I believe it will be successful. Apps like it will be integrated into writing apps in the near future. However, we're still too early for the others. There aren't any (viable) developmental editing tools yet; there are marketing assistance tools but none that are wildly successful for *authors* yet; and there aren't yet any AI tools I know if for authors wanting to write to market. Like I said, it's still early.

Brandon Sanderson Kickstarter. No, not the multi-million dollar one in 2022 that many writers are bitching about (for no real reason other than jealousy). I'm talking about the one Sanderson did in 2020 to create a leather-bound limited edition of one of his novels. I cheered him on then and I'm cheering him on now.

The Fall of Indies. We are currently living in the greatest time in history to be an author. All good things eventually come to an end. What will the transformation of self-publishing into the next era look like? Here's what I wrote:

"I don't know. Global economic recession or depression is my first thought.

"A close second is a trend away from books toward more interactive experiences—gaming, movies, or even virtual reality in the long-term. Authors who don't pivot will be left behind.

"Also, another event that might initiate this is Amazon taking some sort of action that hurts all authors, such as reducing its sales commissions, or restricting the 70% commission to KDP Select authors only, or introducing some sort of new sales commission scheme that drives authors to make less money overall. This happens all the time.

"Another might be a traditional publisher 'comeback.' Maybe the pandemic forces traditional publishers figure out that they need to start innovating and spend a lot of money on technology and marketing value-adds for its authors, enticing more people to seek traditional publishing (and sign the same old terrible contracts). Perhaps innovation technology gives them a clear market advantage over indies, maybe through artificial intelligence. They'll undergo a brand refresh as well.

"It's also not hard to imagine a political event that precipitates a societal distaste for self-publishing, such as a self-published writer who commits a mass murder and leaves behind a trail of books that espouse hatred and very obvious motives. I pray to God that never happens, as it would turn governments and public sentiment against indie writers.

"But honestly, I don't know what an extinction event for

indies would look like, or how bad it would be. It's worth asking the question, as when it happens, it will seem like it came out of nowhere, but will have been glaringly obvious in retrospect."

The fall of indies hasn't happened yet and doesn't appear to be on the horizon, and that's a beautiful thing. However, the concerns I pointed out are still valid. I find myself thinking *a lot* about a traditional publisher comeback. I also find myself thinking a lot about censorship and cancel culture. Earlier in this section, I wrote about governments introducing their own digital currencies so they can track everything you do. In addition to tracking you, they can censor what you buy.

We also seem to be nosediving toward fascism in many countries in the world. In fascism, the language of *everything* is the state. Everything one does must be in service of it. My biggest fear at the time of this writing is that, in my lifetime, the death of the author world as we know it will be due to fascism and governments gatekeeping who can publish and who can't. Traditional publishers could become the state's instrument to do so, and retailers won't do anything to stop it.

A fascist state has no use for an author speaking out against the system. It also has no use for people with active imaginations. The act of writing and the life of intellectualism must be reconditioned in the service of the state in order to survive. That is terrifying, but I don't see how it won't happen, especially in the United States.

I sure hope I'm wrong, but every election cycle, I can't shake the feeling that this may be how the current golden era ends. It won't happen tomorrow, but when it does, it will play out in ways that no one can predict.

How Long Will Smartphones Last? I wrote that smartphones' days are numbered. Hasn't happened yet, thank goodness! I happen to like smartphones a lot and I fail to see the metaverse overtaking them at this time. It will probably happen, though.

That was a fun walk down memory lane. I look forward to seeing how this segment will grow along with the series.

COPYLEFT TROLLS

I read a concerning article from Cory Doctorow about copyleft trolls. The article (which is quite long and detailed but worth reading) details the early days of Creative Commons and a loophole in the standard that attorneys are now exploiting to bleed potential copyright infringers of money. It's far too technical and nuanced to explain in detail here, but before 2008, there is a loophole in Creative Commons licensing where, if you didn't attribute a text correctly, you violated the license, and therefore were subject to a copyright infringement action. The Creative Commons foundation identified this and closed the loophole in 2008, but it still exists for creators and licensees who used the standard before 2008.

As a content creator who regularly relied on Creative Commons early in my career, the article made me nervous. I've written before about trademark trolls and how they could one day bring their evil services to the copyright world. I believe this is how they will do it.

Here's how they operate: they go to media sites that have Creative Commons licenses and use software to scan their databases. They look specifically for works licensed under the old

Creative Commons standard. Then, they scan the internet for any content creators that have attributed the works in question. They then look to see if the attribution is correct. Doctorow points out that many people (even today) still do not attribute Creative Commons works correctly. This was much more so 20 years ago. It's very easy to accidentally do it wrong.

If the attorneys catch even a single typo in the attribution license, they then threaten the content creator with copyright infringement if they don't pay a significant fee. The creator has no choice but to pay. The worst part about all of this is that it is done primarily via software. It is doubtful that there are any attorneys personally reviewing the infringements.

This is precisely what the Creative Commons foundation sought to avoid when they closed this loophole. Upon reading the article, I asked myself (as I always do), "What's my exposure here?"

I don't use Creative Commons anymore, mainly because I prefer to use licensed stock media. It's less risk. Creative Commons has been great for me over the years, but my biggest problem with it has been that some media I have used under a Creative Commons license no longer exists. I don't know if it's because the creator changed their mind or because the media they uploaded wasn't really theirs. I'll never know for sure. That's what scares me. I've always been careful to document any media I use for fear of exactly this type of scenario happening. I keep a spreadsheet that tracks the media I license, where I got it from, a link to the media, and information on the creator.

Doctorow's article helped me identify how I could make the spreadsheet stronger. It also helped me come up with an idea to restructure the spreadsheet so that all the column inputs could be strung together into a formula that gives me the correct Creative Commons attribution every time.

Creative Commons attribution isn't complicated, but it's not intuitive. My exposure is to make sure that whenever I use Creative Commons work that I attribute it correctly. That was my takeaway. I was pretty satisfied with my spreadsheet and very glad that I put it together. I was also glad that I read Doctorow's article because this is an issue that many writers may have to deal with at some point. Many writers can't afford to purchase stock images early in their careers. They use Creative Commons images on their blogs, websites, and even their books. Yet, I don't see very many people talking about this problem.

COLLECTING ADVANTAGES

I've been thinking about advantages lately. In studying the works of successful authors, I've noticed that many of them have advantages that helped them become successful. This is not just true of writers; it's true of successful people in general. There are usually one or two skills that they have or have perfected over the years that contribute to their success.

(I won't talk about survivorship bias here, but that is real. We're just talking philosophically here.)

When I listen to a podcast interview with a successful author, I no longer listen for advice. Much of the advice given anymore is the same.

But when I listen for advantages instead, I take a lot more from the conversation.

For example, I believe that a person's work history can tell you a lot about the skills they have. There's a certain skillset you need to have to be a doctor or military personnel, for example. That's fascinating.

Does that mean that I want to go to medical school or join the navy? No, but it's worth asking the question to figure out what the answer could be. I bet there are lessons you could take away if you studied that profession.

That's just one example of an advantage.

What are my advantages? In other words, what are the skills I have that, when I become successful, people will say are my strengths?

My Work Ethic. I am disciplined and I consistently produce books day in and day out. I also consistently make progress every day toward my writing, rain or shine.

My Sustainability. I have been able to sustain my productivity for the last 10 years with no slowdown in output. In fact, I have gotten faster at producing books over the last 10 years. Burnout isn't in my vocabulary because I'm having fun. I know many authors who could not sustain the pace and volume that I have without burning out.

Prolificality. I am extremely prolific. I am not the most prolific author in the world by any means. I know authors who write circles around me. I consider myself to be a medium-slow author. I'm not too fast, and I'm not too slow, but I'm consistent, which is why I am prolific.

Writing a Book in One Draft. I focus on getting my text down correctly the first time. I don't get hung up on drafting. Therefore, in addition to being consistent, I produce my novels faster than the average author. That is a strategic advantage because it increases the number of books I publish each year.

Alternative Writing Methods. It's no secret that I write on my phone and use dictation to bolster my word counts. (I dictated this very chapter at the sink doing my dishes.) Learning how to write on my phone increased my word counts by 40 percent. Dictation has doubled my word counts, and even tripled it in some cases. And because I write cleanly, I focus on getting my words right the first time. Learning dictation and writing on my phone also has the benefit of helping me write anywhere, anytime, and in any position. It also allows me to continue writing even in the event of an injury or potential disability. That helps me maintain my consistency, which helps me maintain my prolific status.

Advanced Editing. I have an editor who works quickly and turns around my manuscripts faster than the industry average. That's an advantage. I also use editing macros in Microsoft Word to help me catch common errors that my editor would have caught. This results in cleaner manuscripts, which will reduce my editing costs and improve the quality of my work. I also have developed a framework of thinking about my editing in terms of data and analytics; this has helped me to identify true weaknesses in my writing and shore them up accordingly.

Format Parity. By the end of this year, I will be in the position to publish the ebook, paperback, hardcover, and large print editions of my books on day one. The more formats you publish and the earlier you publish them, the more long-term earning potential you have.

Audiobooks. I'm still not at the point in my career where I can afford to produce audiobook versions of all of my books. However, I have enough titles in audio that it is a lucrative investment for me. As I become more successful, I look forward to the day when I will be able to release the audiobook edition very quickly after my other formats. Some authors have developed a workflow where they will produce the audiobook and launch it on day one, but I don't agree with that philosophy because you can spend a lot of time waiting for your audiobooks. As soon as a book is ready, I would much rather publish it. You can always let your readers know about the audiobook later, and that serves as good marketing because you're continuing to make people aware that your book exists. But sure, there is definitely a time and place for launching your audiobooks on day one.

Narrating My Own Audiobooks. In the future, when I am in a better position to do so, I would love to be able to narrate many of my audiobooks. If I did that, then I probably *could* release the audiobook on day one. Narrating your own audiobook is a place where even angels fear to tread, so this is something that makes me stand out. I narrated the audio version of 150 *Self-Publishing Questions Answered*, so I know the process of producing an audiobook and I know how to do it quickly and correctly. Hell, I passed Audible's and Findaway Voices' QA standards on my first try!

Being "Wide." I am not a fan of Kindle Unlimited. I have used it over the years, and I've made money with it for the years, but I don't believe it is a sustainable strategy if you want to have a long-term career. While I have dabbled with Kindle Unlimited in KDP Select over the years, at the time of this writing, 100 percent of my titles are available wide. Readers can buy any of my books anywhere and in whatever format they desire. I wish my Apple, Google, and Kobo sales were a little higher, but they have been increasing over the years. What matters is that readers can find my books on those platforms. This way, if I have a breakout success, readers will have over 80 books in my portfolio to choose from. In a decade, that number will be much higher.

Podcasting and Video. I have been a podcaster and YouTuber since 2014. That has helped my writing and my marketing tremendously. I'm well-recognized in the indie author space, I'm always in demand for interviews, and I like to think that I deliver a good interview when I show up. Because I constantly teach writing concepts, I can express them simply and in a way that sounds good in audio and video formats. If I become far more successful than I am now, this will be to my benefit because it will help me sell more books and connect with more readers. Most importantly, perhaps, the advice I'm giving will help more people.

Law School. I went to law school and have education on contracts, copyright, and other legal topics. This is an advantage, even though I will never be a practicing lawyer (or qualified to be one). But I know how to think like a lawyer, and that's valuable.

Work History. Insurance turned out to be a good career for me and my writing. I have specialized in general liability, which means that I understand the dangers that businesses face every day. I also know how to avoid some of these dangers. My particular line of work has also helped me develop additional skills such as data analysis, advanced Microsoft Excel skills, public speaking, and more.

Automatic Sales Insights. In 2020, I discussed my process of automating the aggregation of my sales reports. At the click of a button, I can run all of my sales reports through a workflow that adds up all of the sales for all of my titles into a single report that I can use to mine for insights. For example, I can tell you to the penny how much money I made from my book sales in Germany across all retailers in all formats in the second quarter of 2015. That's powerful, and I use this data to drive my marketing decisions.

Consistent Cover Branding. In 2017, I embarked on a journey to rebrand my titles under a unified pen name design. Most of my Michael La Ronn covers have my name in big letters in the same font. This way, if you look at one of my titles, you know it's one of my titles. Ten years from now, when I have a significantly larger fiction portfolio, this will magnify my brand. It's still amazing how few authors do this.

Fan-mail. Anyone who has filled out my contact form knows that I respond to emails quickly. I receive a lot of fan-mail, and I make it a priority to respond to my fans. Even if people are asking simple questions that I've received a thousand times, I still take the time to respond.

Why do I do it? First, because I care. The people reaching out are usually struggling with some aspect of writing, and I have always tried to never lose sight of the struggles I had when I was an aspiring writer. I understand the emotions, the mindset, and the struggles. If I can help somebody in a small way, I see this as paying it forward.

Second, more practically, it keeps me in touch with what people are struggling with. It also helps me determine if the advice I'm giving is actually helpful or if I need to re-tweak it. I can use those personal one-on-one interactions to help my audience at large.

Third, it's good marketing. A reader reaching out asking me about one of my fantasy series and receiving a prompt response has the potential to become a fan for life.

Fourth, almost no one else in the writing space does it, especially when they get over a certain level. I don't want to become one of those writers. I like to think that, even if I reach a point where I receive a thousand pieces of fan-mail a day, that I would be able to find a system to answer all of those people's questions personally, whether it be from me or an assistant.

Fan-mail always deserves a personal response. If someone spends their hard-earned money on your book, and your book moved them to the point of typing a beautiful email, then that person deserves a response. I write about this in my book *The Reader's Bill of Rights*—check it out if you're interested.

I hope this chapter didn't come across as too vain. That's not my intent. I just want to reflect on some of my strengths. I encourage you to do the same. I also encourage you to look at the strengths of other successful indie authors. You may be able to learn from them; you may also realize a strength in them that you have in yourself but are not realizing yet. That's the most beautiful type of self-discovery because it connects you with who you are meant to be.

I believe advantages are worth studying for that reason alone.

WHY YOU ARE YOUR OWN WORST ENEMY

I recently watched a YouTube video called "Nietzsche - You Are Your Own Worst Enemy" on the Freedom in Thought YouTube channel (published August 12, 2021). This eight-minute video perfectly explained why you are the biggest obstacle to your success.

Your biggest enemy is you. Not marketing. Not learning the craft of writing. Not learning business. But you.

I highly recommend that you look at the video and watch it for yourself, but I will attempt to summarize the main idea. The YouTube channel is a philosophy channel that summarizes the ideas of the world's greatest philosophers.

The video is a dialogue between an acrobat and a circus master. The acrobat wants to become a famous acrobat but doesn't feel that he can because society doesn't value artists and his family will think less of him for pursuing this profession.

The master takes him to task and explains that:

- fears arise from your thoughts.
- thoughts arise from your desires.

Therefore, it could be said that your desires lead to your thoughts, which lead to your fears.

The master explains that the young acrobat wants society to value artists and he wants to get paid. But his fears and thoughts are holding him back.

However, you can't change your desires. Instead, they fall away on their own through understanding. Therefore, if you seek to understand a problem on a new level, you can change your thinking, which will change your fears, possibly eliminate them.

To assuage the acrobat's fears about society not valuing artists, the master explains that people will value anything that is a necessity. If the things you create are a necessity, then people will pay for them. He also explains that people respect you when you live according to their values. If you live according to your own values, then there will always be people in the world who don't respect you, but you will attract the right people into your life. If you don't do that, you will become resentful and regret the choices you have made in your life.

Wow. Such a powerful message in just an eight-minute video.

I wish I could do the video proper justice, but my main take-away was the premise of the video: your fears arise from your thoughts, which arise from your desires. Change your desires through understanding of yourself and your world and you will change your life. That's a philosophy to live by.

FEEDING THE INSATIABLE WRITING BEAST

I am on a journey to publish 100 books by the end of 2023. I began this journey in 2012, and I'm looking forward to putting my number of published books in the triple digits soon.

It takes a lot of time, energy, and effort to accomplish a feat like this. It is the result of many early mornings, late nights, time alone at my desk, and discipline, dedication, and commitment.

What happens after I achieve 100 books?

I'll want 200 books, and after that, 400. And after that, if I'm lucky—1000 books.

I have realized that I must be careful in this pursuit. It is an insatiable beast that must always be fed. No matter what I do, I will always want to increase the number. If I'm not careful, this could be akin to playing with fire.

I have known several authors who wrote at a breakneck pace only to burn out, negating any progress they made. Burnout scares me, but I have never thought that it was an issue for me. The best vaccines against burnout are to have fun, take care of yourself, and stay connected with why you are writing in the first place. You should know enough about me to know that I don't have any problems in any of those areas.

But still, I have become more aware of the writing beast in the lead-up to accomplishing my goal of 100 books. I also need to be reading, marketing, and doing things that will help me run a viable and profitable writing business. If I focus too much on productivity, I risk throwing all of the other elements of my writing business out of kilter.

But let me tell you something: there is nothing like feeding the beast. I love preparing a novel for publication, hitting that publish button, and watching the counter go up.

My theory is that there is a big marketing difference in saying that you have published 100 books versus anything in the two digits. People are always impressed when you have published one book. They are *really* impressed when you have published in the double digits. Their heads explode once you get over 50. Publishing over 100 books is simply unfathomable for most people; publishing 1000 books is otherworldly, and, dare I say it, a little suspicious to most people.

My point is that I don't think there will be that much of a difference in people's reaction moving forward once I have passed 100 books. Whether the number is 100, 200, or 999, the reaction will be the same type of bewilderment.

I would love to surpass the 1000 book mark, but I highly doubt that will happen. Therefore, I will have to be comfortable with three digits for a long time, which I most definitely will be.

What should my priorities be after publishing 100 books?

First, I don't intend to slow down. I do, however, plan to introduce more things into my daily routine to ground me, like reading more. I still read many times more books each year than the average person, but I could be reading more. And I will.

Ultimately, I don't want to fall prey to the writing beast. In my book *The Indie Author Bestiary*, I write about burnout and the many other beasts of the writing world. I'm very much aware of the impact they can have in your life.

In the meantime, I'm going to race for 100 and then reevaluate once I have achieved that milestone.

Q2 2022 STRATEGY PROGRESS

I'm now halfway through 2022. It has been a good year so far. Here is the progress I've made toward my goals.

BECOME A WORLD-CLASS CONTENT CREATOR

To achieve my goal of becoming a world-class content creator, I will focus on the following tactical priorities:
- Demonstrate a commitment to learning the craft of storytelling and teaching
- Demonstrate a commitment to outstanding quality AND quantity

Examples of day-to-day activities that will help me carry out my tactical priorities include:
- Keep learning through online courses and workshops taught by professional writers who are further down the path I want to write
- Reading
- Developing mentorships

•Finding new ways to increase my daily word counts

•Mastering different writing methods

•Documenting my process of becoming a successful writer in the *Indie Author Confidential* series

•Cleaning up my platform to ensure a consistent quality reader experience

What did I do to become a world-class content creator during Q2 2022?

- I have taken approximately 20 workshops from Dean Wesley Smith and Kristine Kathryn Rusch on writing craft.
- I have read (and studied the craft in) 20 books so far this year.
- I am still on track to publish 100 books by end of 2023.
- I exploded my dictation word counts by purchasing a voice recorder and implementing some hacks to help me dictate and transcribe more cleanly.
- I improved my fiction editing benchmark to 1 edit per 300 words, which represents a 3x improvement over my writing in 2018, which was 1 edit per 110 words.
- I rebranded *The Good Necromancer* and *The Chicago Rat Shifter* series under Michael La Ronn, concentrating my urban fantasy footprint. I also renamed my *Magic Trackers* series to *The Dream Mage* to improve its standing in the portfolio.
- I licensed the ebook version of *The Author Estate Handbook* and *The Author Heir Handbook* to The Alliance of Independent Authors. Later this year, it will be available as a free download to ALLi members as part of their membership. The ebook is

licensed as a special edition and it doesn't impede on my rights in the least. This will make the books available to a global audience and expand my reach.

BECOME A TECHNOLOGY AND DATA-DRIVEN WRITER

To achieve my goal of becoming a technology and data-driven writer, I will focus on the following tactical priorities:

•Use technology to make the business more efficient

•Use data to get insights

Examples of day-to-day activities that will help me carry out my tactical priorities include:

•Developing a tax plan

•Developing an estate plan assisted with technology

•Learning how to design my own covers

•Hiring a personal assistant for small tasks where it makes sense

•Developing a metadata database for my work

•Improving my readers' experience on my website

•Implementing direct sales for my fiction

What did I do to become a more technology and data-driven writer during Q2 2022?

1. I implemented my tax strategy and it worked very well.
2. I continued to take steps with my estate planning.
3. I took the first steps in learning how to design my own book covers.
4. I made some minor improvements to my website, making it a little easier for readers to find works they will enjoy.

5. I successfully implemented direct sales for my fiction.
6. I began doing "deep quality checks" for a handful of titles in my portfolio to double-check that they were uploaded correctly. A deep check includes reviewing the work on all the retailer dashboards, something I don't do during my normal QA process.
7. Signed up for Kindle Trends to get insights into the urban fantasy genre.

2022 is still off to a great start. Next quarter, I will continue doing more of the same: focusing on growing my portfolio to 100 titles and focusing on maximizing the value of my portfolio through new formats and quality assessments.

As I said at the end of 2021, 2022 is the final year for me to get my fundamentals right. I'm excited about that, and I'm looking forward to what the next quarter brings.

CONTENT CREATED WHILE WRITING THIS BOOK

This section recaps the books I've published and media I've created during the quarter. To keep the book evergreen, I will not include links to podcasts or magazine articles because sometimes links break over time, especially with podcasts if the hosts stop podcasting. You can easily search for them to see if they're still active at the time you're reading this book. If they are, enjoy! If not, please accept my apologies.

Books

The Dream Mage (formerly Magic Trackers)
New name, same great characters and story!
Aisha Robinson is a dream mage. She can read your dreams and even jump into your mind and control what you dream about. She's built a business helping people unravel their dreams so they can solve their problems. Join her and her cousins as they keep people safe from dream-eating demons.
Buy at www.michaellaronn.com/dreammage.

. . .

The Good Necromancer Series

Follow the adventures of Lester Broussard, necromancer extraordinaire who uses his powers for good. Talking to the dead and controlling them are Lester's specialties, and he does them to keep the city of St. Louis safe from evil demons and other things that go bump in the night.

Buy at www.michaellaronn.com/thegoodnecromancer.

The Chicago Rat Shifter Series

Meet Cyrus Grant, rat shifter. After a bad breakup, getting turned into a rat is the last thing he needs. Now he must survive the brutal world of rats under the city of Chicago. Sometimes, big heroes come in small packages.

Buy at www.michaellaronn.com/ratshifter.

Podcast/Video Appearances

"How to Balance Writing with a Busy Lifestyle" on The Self-Publishing Show

In this interview, Michael talks about building a writing business while raising a family, working a full-time job, and attending law school classes in the evenings.

"Estate Planning for Authors with Michael La Ronn" on The Indy Author Podcast

Michael talks about estate planning essentials and not-so-obvious pitfalls that are waiting for authors' heirs.

CAN YOU KEEP A SECRET?

If you liked the ideas in this book, check out the rest of the volumes in the series at www.authorlevelup.com/confidential.

MEET M.L. RONN

Science fiction and fantasy on the wild side!

M.L. Ronn (Michael La Ronn) is the author of many science fiction and fantasy novels including *The Good Necromancer*, *Android X,* and *The Last Dragon Lord* series.

In 2012, a life-threatening illness made him realize that storytelling was his #1 passion. He's devoted his life to writing ever since, making up whatever story makes him fall out of his chair laughing the hardest. Every day.

Learn more about Michael
www.authorlevelup.com (for writers)
www.michaellaronn.com (fiction)

MORE BOOKS BY M.L. RONN

Books for Writers

Indie Author Confidential (Series)
    How to Write Your First Novel
    Be a Writing Machine
    Mental Models for Writers
    The Indie Writer's Encyclopedia
    The Indie Author Atlas
    The Indie Author Bestiary
    The Reader's Bill of Rights
    The Self-Publishing Compendium
    150 Self-Publishing Questions Answered
    Authors, Steal This Book
    The Indie Author Strategy Guide
    How to Dictate a Book
    Advanced Author Editing
    Keep Your Books Selling
    The Author Estate Handbook
    The Author Heir Handbook

Interactive Fiction: How to Engage Readers and Push the Boundaries of Story Telling
Indie Poet Rock Star
Indie Poet Formatting
2016 Indie Author State of the Union

More Books for Writers:

www.authorlevelup.com/books

Fiction:
www.michaellaronn.com/books